A Sunshine Garden Doll Pattern

I0108350

Rosemary

By Anne Cote

Rosemary

For more Sunshine Garden Dolls Patterns
Visit bluedaisyzone.com

Daisy

Sunflower

Poppy   Dandelion   Marigold   Rosemary   Sage   Primrose

ISBN-13: 978-1-940354-68-2

Copyright © 2021 by Anne Cote

All rights reserved. No part of this book may be reproduced in any form by any electronic or mechanical means, including photocopying, recording, or information storage and retrieval without permission in writing from the copyright owner.

This book includes pattern templates that may be used for the original creation of the doll and any creative changes desired by the crafter. The templates themselves cannot be reproduced or sold in the original form.

Text, Photos, and Illustrations by Anne Cote
Cover Design by Anne Cote & Layne Walker
Edited by Joan Cote and Layne Walker

First edition published in January 2021
Published by New Friends Publishing, LLC
Lake Havasu City, AZ

Visit New Friends Publishing's Website at
www.newfriendspublishing.com

CONTENTS

To

All Crafters

whose Creations

bring Joy to Others

Materials for Rosemary

Rosemary is full of fun and energy. She likes to laugh with her friends and tease her twin brother Sage (pattern sold separately). She is 20" tall. She wears bright, sunny clothes to match her fun-loving attitude.

SUPPLIES

There are lots of options for materials, including scraps of fabric and fancy trims. I've listed the products I use in brackets. Other options abound and are listed below.

DOLL

44"x13" cotton fabric for body
Craft paint, markers
    [Anita's Acrylic White for whites of eyes and dots in the eyes]
    [Sharpie Permanent Markers for eyes, nose, brows, lashes, mouth]
Yarn for hair [Yarn Bee Fleece Lite: "Black"]
Poly-fil Stuffing 6-8 oz.
Stuffing tools [tube and stick]
Fabric turning tools [tube and stick, see instructions]

CLOTHING

44"x19" cotton floral fabric for bloomers, top, and skirt
9"x9" contrasting felt for vest
32"x3 1/2" cotton fabric for hair bow
12"x8" black felt for shoes

30" 1/2"-1" lace trim (flat or gathered) for skirt
18" 1/2"-1" lace trim (flat or gathered) for bloomers
11" 1/2"-1" lace trim (flat or gathered) for neckline
11" 1/2"-1" lace trim (flat or gathered) for sleeves
    (Total trim: 70")

18" 1/4" elastic for bloomers and skirt
2 snap fasteners for top
2 1/2" buttons for vest
General sewing supplies

OPTIONS

Face can be painted, embroidered, or drawn on with permanent markers.
Bloomers in a contrasting color takes 20"x10" of fabric.
Top in contrasting color takes 26"x7" of fabric.
Skirt in contrasting color takes 32"x11" of fabric.
Hair instructions are for hand sewing. Glue can be used instead, or a combination of sewing and glue.
Hair Bow can be made with bias tape or ribbon, rather than cut and sewn.
Trim can be flat or gathered.
Snaps can be plastic or metal or replaced by buttons.

www.bluedaisyzone.com
©2021, Blue Daisy Zone, LLC

COPYRIGHT and CHILD SAFETY

COPYRIGHT

What **CAN** you do? You **CAN** sell the items that you make from this pattern. You can use the templates to create the doll. You can also add your own artistic flare to what you create when using the templates. What you make is your property and is yours to do with as you wish.

What **CAN'T** you do? You **CANNOT** copy the pattern illustrations, diagrams, written instructions or photos. You cannot simply photocopy, scan, or reproduce the sewing pattern in any way and then sell copies of it. This is an infringement of copyright laws.

CHILD SAFETY

This doll is advised for children 3 years or older. For a younger child or baby, bows, sashes, ribbons, or any loose parts should be removed or sewn securely onto the doll or clothing. Fancy laces can wear out with use and separate from the clothing. They are preferable for children over 3. Plastic baby snaps can be used instead of metal snaps. The pattern calls for painting the face. Embroidery and painting are safety measures. Buttons should not be used for eyes for small children. I cannot be responsible for the way each crafter uses these patterns or instructions. Please consider the age of the child for which you are making the doll.

For more information on copyright laws and safety information, there is a great amount of information on the internet. For pattern questions, please send an email to Anne at this address: bluedaisyzone@gmail.com

Website: bluedaisyzone.com

© 2021, Blue Daisy Zone, LLC All Rights Reserved

Making the Doll

All seam allowances are 1/4 inch.

Use a small machine stich for more stability.

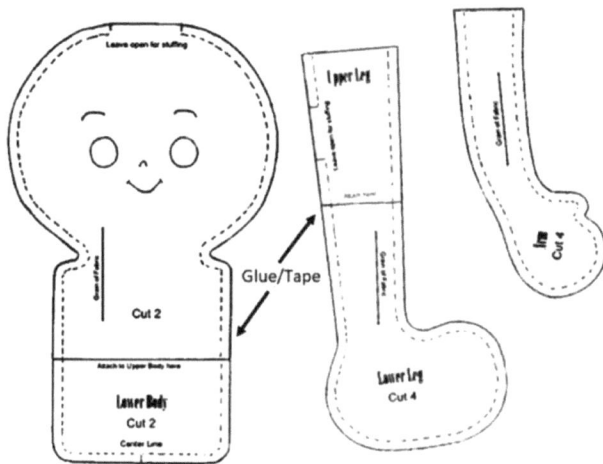

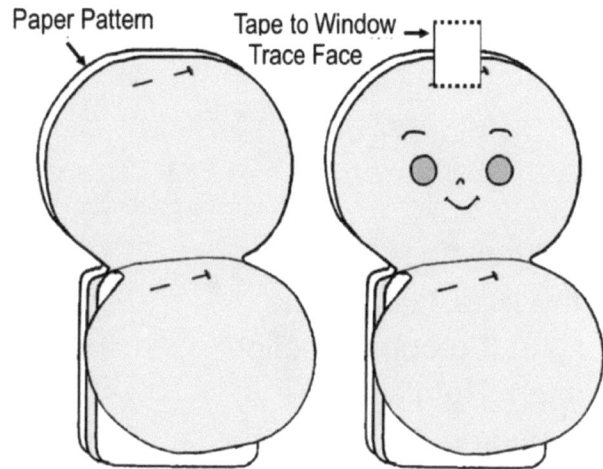

Cut out the patterns. Glue or tape the leg and body pieces together where indicated. Pin to fabric and cut out pieces.

FACE: Lay the fabric head/body on top of the paper pattern. Pin one side of the fabric head to the pattern top. Pin the folded layer of fabric to the lower body. Tape or hold the head/body to a window or lightbox and trace the face with pencil.

All the features can be painted or embroidered. For Rosemary, I used Sharpie Permanent Markers for all the features except for the white acrylic paint for the whites of the eyes and the dots on the eyes.

Rosemary's eyes, lashes, and brows are black. Her nose can be black or dark brown. Her mouth is red.

Leave Open

Clip

Reinforce
Curve

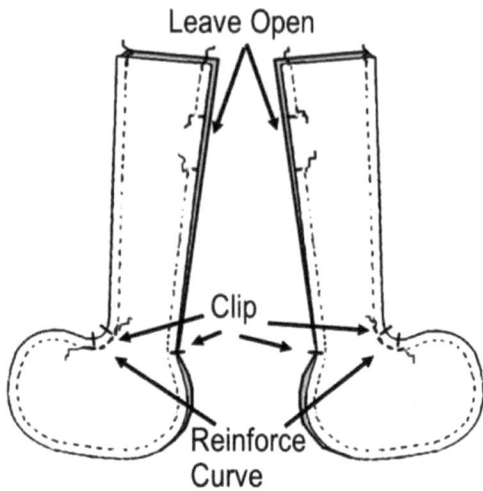

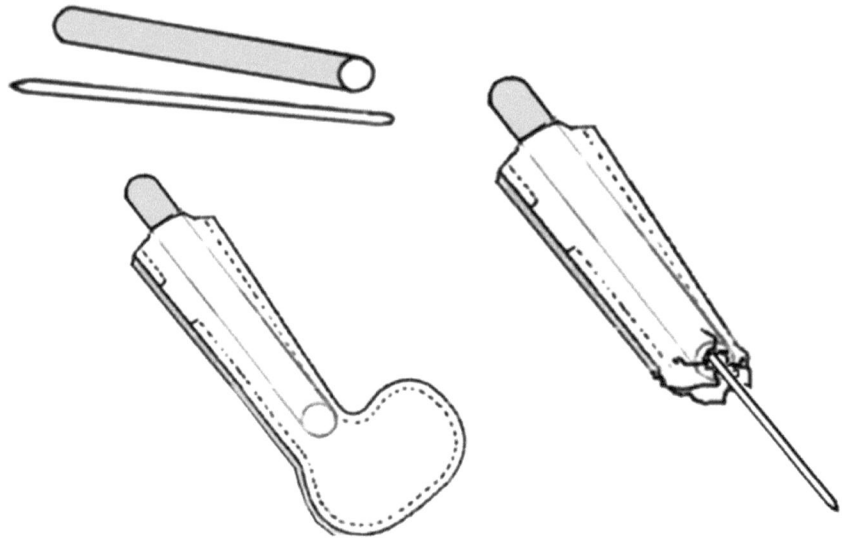

LEGS: Right sides together, stitch the legs, leaving the opening in the upper section for stuffing. Reinforce the curve between the top of the foot and leg. Clip curves.

Turn the legs right side out. My favorite way of turning narrow fabric pieces is with a tube and stick. In this case, push the tube inside the leg. With the stick, push the foot into the tube until it comes out the other end.

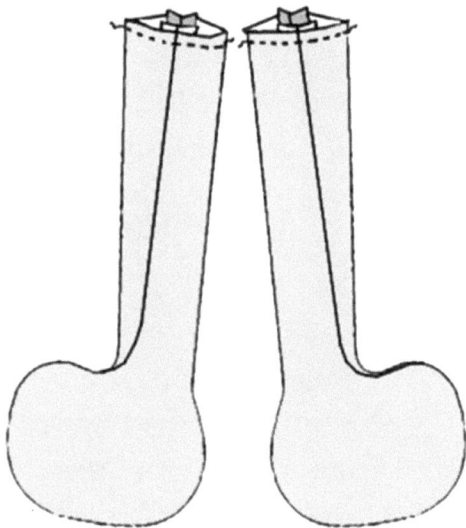

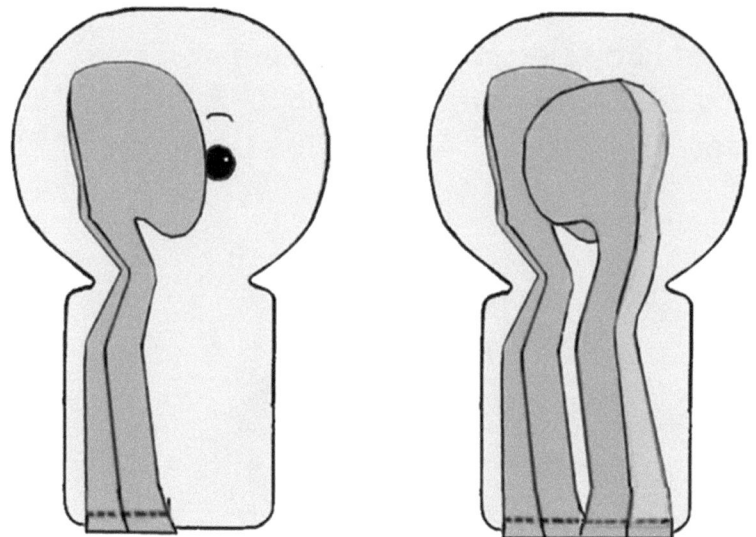

Open the top of the legs and pin the seams together. Baste across the top.

Place the top of the legs on the bottom of the right side of the body with the face. It's very important that the toes face the features on the face. Otherwise, the feet and legs will come out backwards. The leg tops should lie 1/4 inch from the side of the body on both sides. The legs should hang just below the body about 1/8 inch to make sure they are caught in the stitches. The legs might overlap a little in the middle. Pin/baste the legs in place along the bottom of the body.

Leave Open

Clip

Reinforce Neck Curve

Ladder Stitch

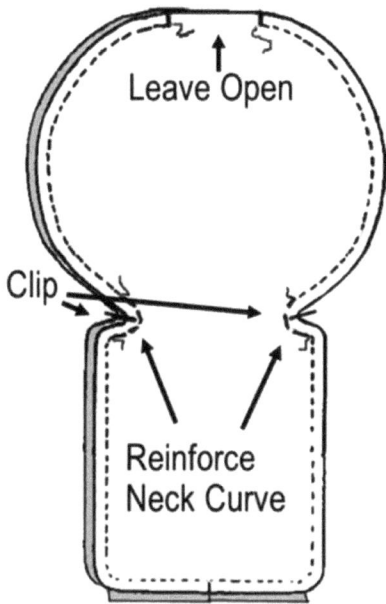

BODY: Right sides together, pin/baste the entire body, making sure the feet and legs are not caught in the seam allowance. Starting at the head, stitch around the entire body, leaving the opening for the stuffing. Reinforce the neck area with extra stitches. Clip the curves.

Turn the body right side out. Stuff the body and head. Sew the head closed with a ladder stitch as shown above.

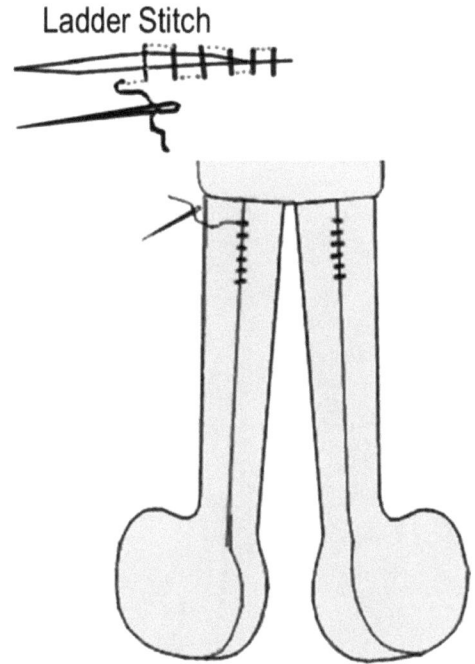

On the back side, stuff the legs. Close the legs with a ladder stitch.

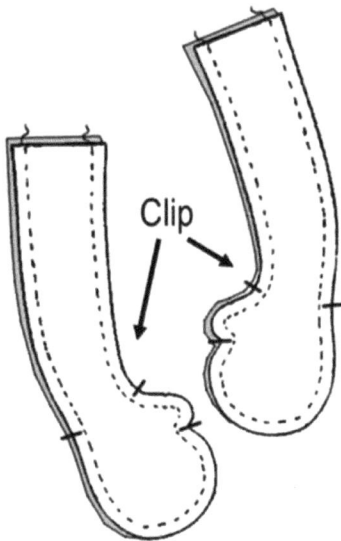

Overcast Stitch

Clip

ARMS: Right sides together, stitch the arms. Clip curves. Turn right side out.

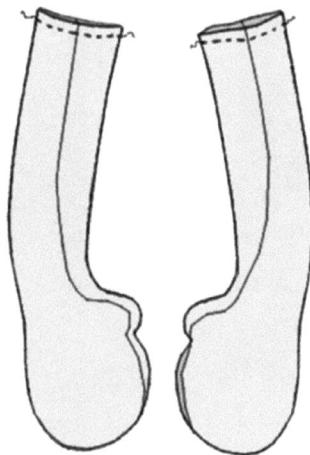

Stuff the arms to about 1 inch from the top. Turn the top edge inside 1/4 inch and pin closed. Hand sew or machine stitch closed.

Pin arms to shoulders. Stitch by hand with an overcast stitch.

Making the Hair

Please read all the instructions before starting the hair.
Rosemary has two layers of hair plus bangs.

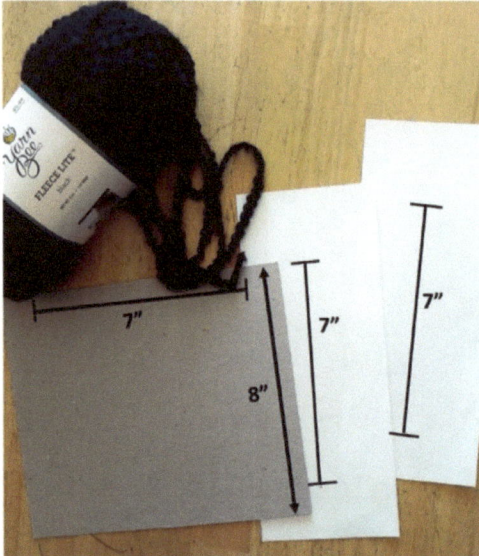

1. Preparation: For the hair, divide a piece of white copy paper into two pieces. (You can use stabilizer material instead if you wish.) Draw a 7-inch line down the middle of each piece. This will form the sewing lines to hold the yarn together. For wrapping the yarn, you will need a piece of cardboard that is 8 inches long by at least 7 inches wide.

2. Wrap the yarn 80 times around the 8-inch side of the cardboard. The width of the yarn should stretch across 7 inches at the top.

3. Place a piece masking tape across the yarn about 1 inch from the top. Do this on both sides of the cardboard to hold the yarn together. With a scissors, cut along the bottom edge to separate strands.

Tape both sides

7" line off-centered between tape

Seam

4. Carefully move yarn to one of the papers, lining the tape up with the 7-inch line, off-centered to the left about 1/2 inch. The off-centered seam will create a layered look when placed on the doll.

5. Stitch the yarn close to the left side. Use a small stitch, which will create more perforations in the paper, making it easier remove. Remove the tape and the paper.

Seam folded here.

6, When folding the yarn at the seam, one layer should be shorter than the other. When placing the yarn on the doll, the shorter side should be on top. (Hard to see the top layer in the photo with the dark yarn. The white line shows where the shorter layer falls.)

Repeat Steps 2 to 5 for the second piece of hair.

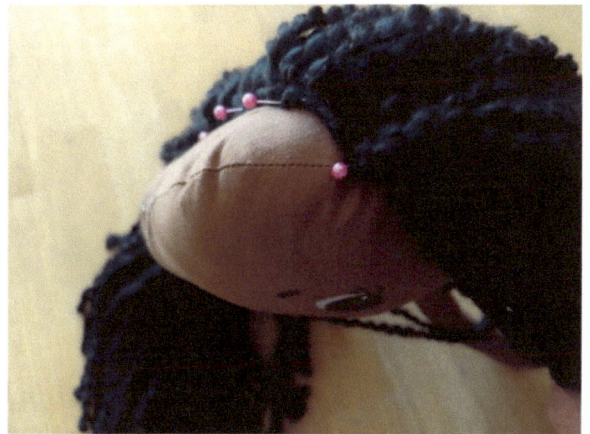

7. Pin one yarn piece across the back of the doll's head about 1 inch below the top of the head. The yarn should wrap around the sides of the doll's head and stop about 1/4 inch in front of the side seam. Fold under any extra yarn.

8. Use a matching thread with an overcast stitch to attach the yarn to the head.

9. Center the second section of hair across the head just in front of the seam line. Make sure the shorter layer of the yarn is on top for the layered look. Pin in place. Use an overcast stitch to attach to the head.

Slip off folded cardboard

10. For bangs, use a light piece of cardboard 3 inches by at least 5½ inches. Cardboard should bend a little down the long side. Prepare a piece of copy paper (or stabilizer) with a 5½-inch line for seam.

5½"

5½"

3"

11. Loosely wrap the yarn around the 3-inch side of the cardboard 40 times and cover 5½ inches across the top. Place masking tape about 1/2 inch on both sides. Fold the cardboard slightly and carefully slip the yarn off the cardboard. Do not cut the yarn.

12. Place taped yarn on the paper, lining up the center of the yarn with the line on the paper. Sew a seam down center of yarn. Push yarn under needle as sewing. Remove tape and paper.

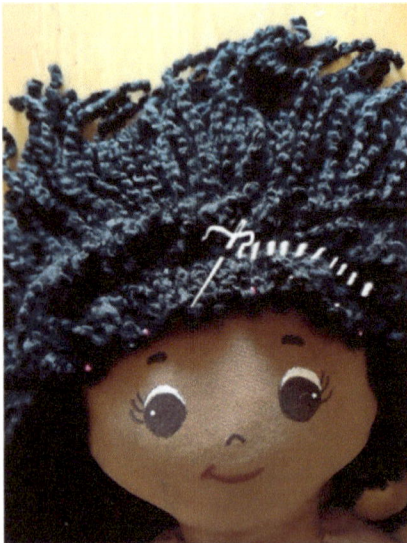

13. Center the bangs over the front of the face with the seam lying open just in front of the hair line. Pin and use an overcast stitch along the seam to attach the bangs to the head.

14. Shake the head a little to allow the back of the hair to fall naturally into a shaggy look. Trim along the bottom to even out the hair. Trim some of the layers to create more of a layered look.

Making the Clothes

All seam allowances are 1/4 inch.

Cut out paper pattern and glue/tape Skirt Front to Skirt Back. Cut out the fabric.

All edges can be finished by using an overstitch or making a tiny fold inward on the edge of the fabric. I use a pinking shears to cut out my pattern pieces and leave this as my finished edge.

Bloomers

Clip

Insert Elastic on Safety Pin

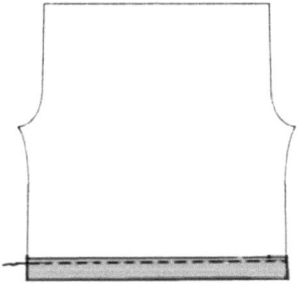

Press the lower edge of bloomers under 1/4 inch then another 1/2 inch to form elastic casing. Stitch close to hem edge.

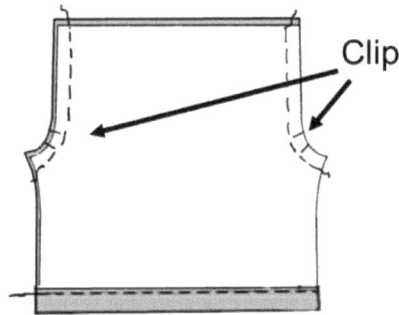

With right sides together, stitch the crotch seams. Clip curves.

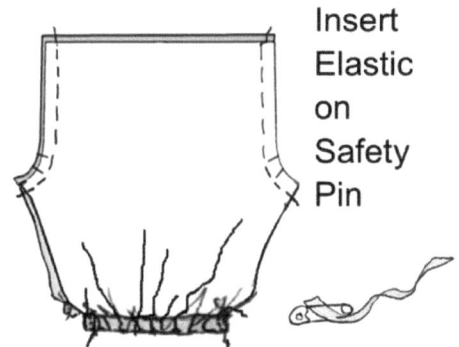

Insert a 5-inch piece of elastic on a safety pin into one end of casing. Push pin in until 1/8 inch of elastic is exposed outside seam. Stitch to hold in place. Push pin through to other end. Leave 1/8 inch outside casing. Remove pin.

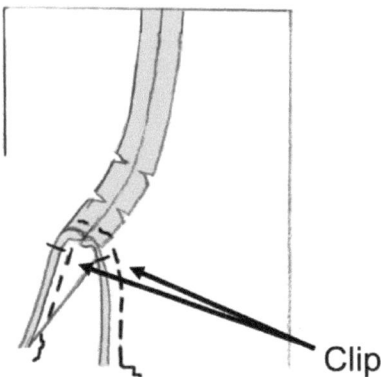

Leave open

Clip

Stitch closed

Right sides together, stitch leg seams from crotch to leg bottoms going through elastic. Clip curves near crotch. Press seam open.

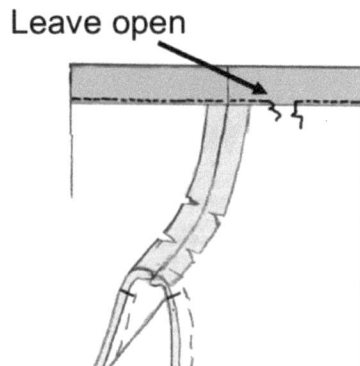

Fold top edge over 1/4 inch then another 1/2 inch to form casing for elastic. Press. Stitch near lower edge. Leave a section open for inserting elastic.

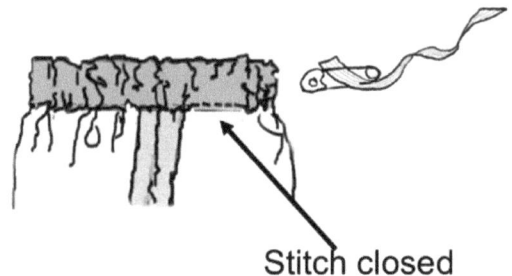

Cut 9 inches of elastic. Insert into the casing on a safety pin. Push pin through to the other side. Overlap the elastic 1/4 inch. Stitch elastic together securely. By hand or machine, stitch the casing closed.

Top

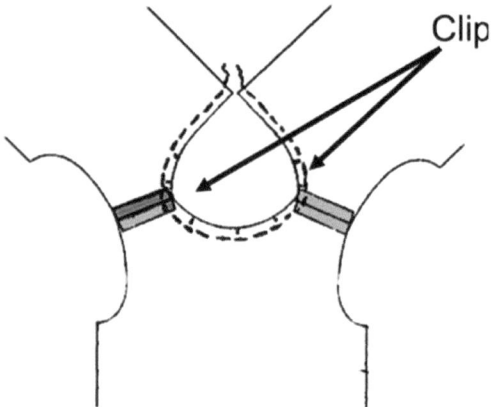

Right bodice sides together, stitch shoulder seams. Press seams open. Stay-stitch around neck to give it stability. Clip curves.

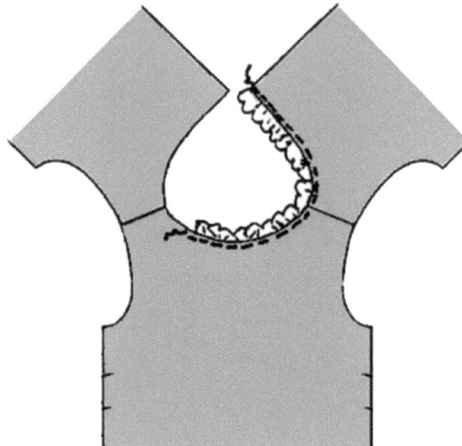

Press neck edge under at stay-stitching. Pin/baste trim to neck and stitch. Trim can be sewn on inside or outside of fabric, depending on preference or on the finished edge of the trim.

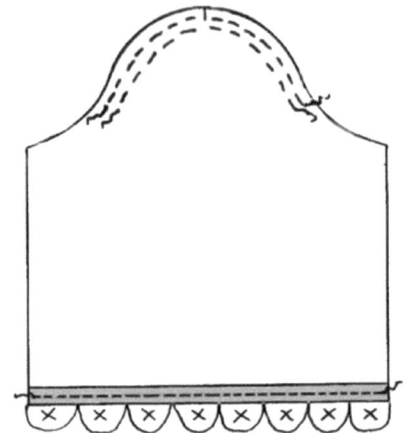

Make two rows of a running stitch at the top of the sleeve for gathering. Press the lower edge under 1/4 inch. Pin/baste trim and stitch.

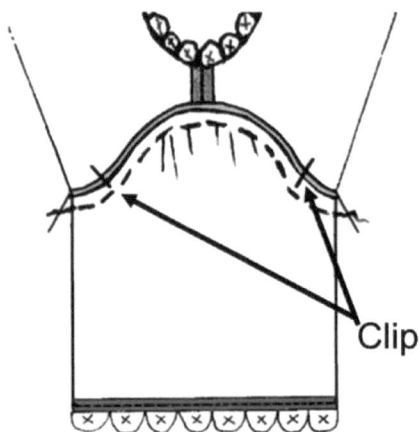

Right sides together, match center of sleeve to the shoulder seam. Pull up gathering threads to fit armhole. Pin/baste sleeve to armhole and stitch. Clip curves.

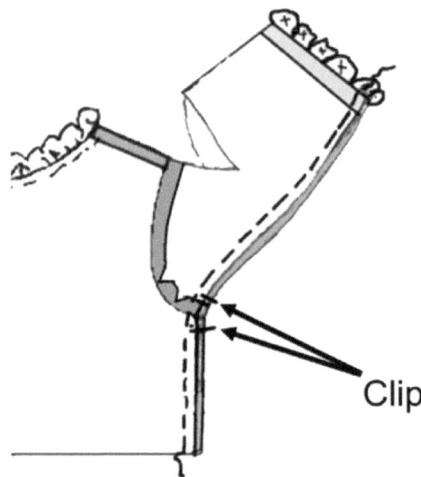

Fold armhole seam toward sleeve. Pin/baste and stitch the underarm seams from the bodice to the end of the sleeve trim. Clip curves where bodice and sleeve meet.

Press lower edge under 1/4 inch, then another 1/4 inch to form hem. Stitch.

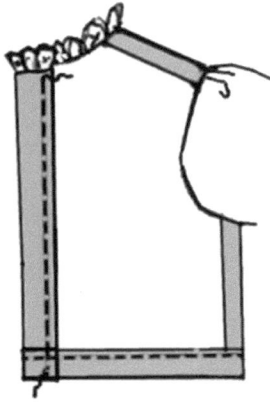

Fold facing over wrong side of bodice. Press and stitch.

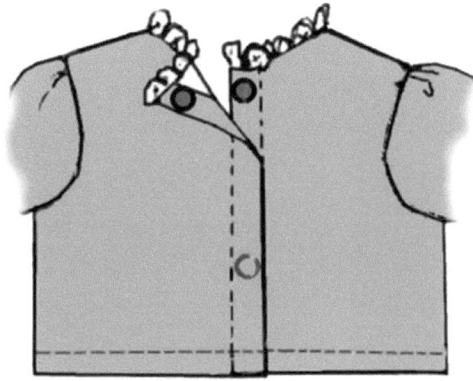

Overlap the left side on top of the right side. Attach snaps to top of bodice and below middle of bodice.

Skirt

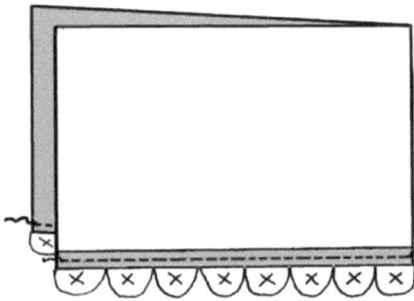

Fold bottom edge under 1/4 inch. Press. Pin/baste trim and stitch.

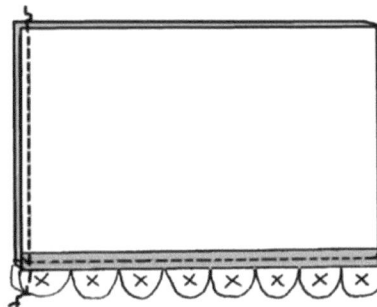

Right sides together, pin and stitch back seam.

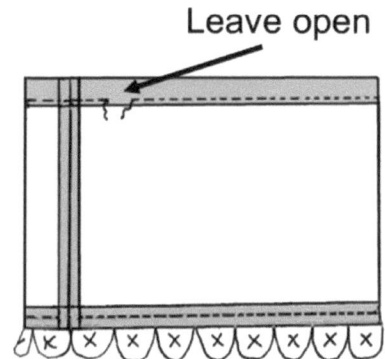

Leave open

Fold top edge over 1/4 inch, then another 1/2 inch to form casing for elastic. Press and stitch near lower edge. Leave a section open to insert the elastic.

Insert Elastic on Safety Pin

Cut 9 inches of elastic. Insert into the casing on a safety pin. Push pin through to the other side. Overlap the elastic 1/4 inch and stitch elastic together securely. By hand or machine, stitch the casing closed.

Stitch closed

Vest

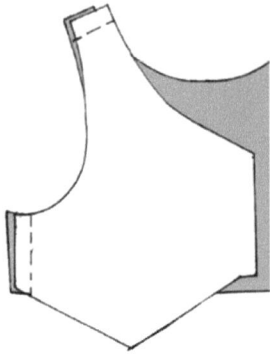

Right sides together, stitch shoulder seams and side seams. Press seam open with fingers.

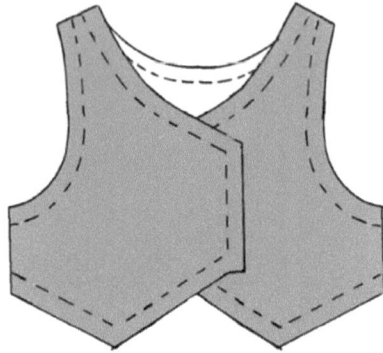

Top-stitch 1/4 inch around entire vest and arm holes to stabilize the felt. Use a matching or contrasting thread.

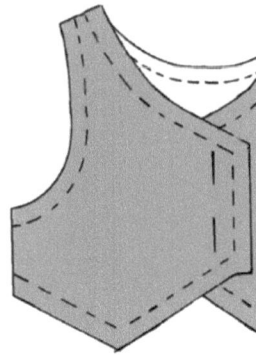

Make small slits on the right side of the vest front for buttonholes.

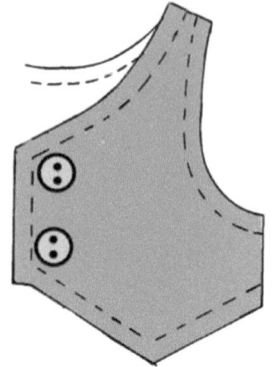

On the left side of the vest front, sew two buttons.

Hair Bow

Leave Open

Clip Corners

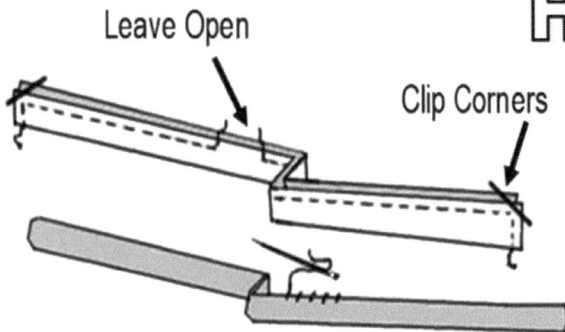

Cut one piece of fabric 32"x3½". Fold the fabric in half longwise. Pin and stitch, starting from each end and leaving about a 1-inch opening near the middle. Clip corners and turn right side out. Close the open section with an overcast stitch.

Shoes

Reinforce

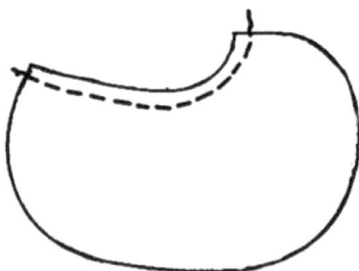

On each shoe piece, stay-stitch along top edge for stability.

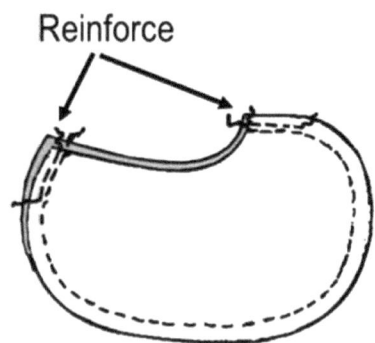

With right sides together, stitch from toe to back of heel. Reinforce beginning and ending with extra stitches for stability.

Patterns
For
Doll and Clothing

Patterns can be cut out or traced.

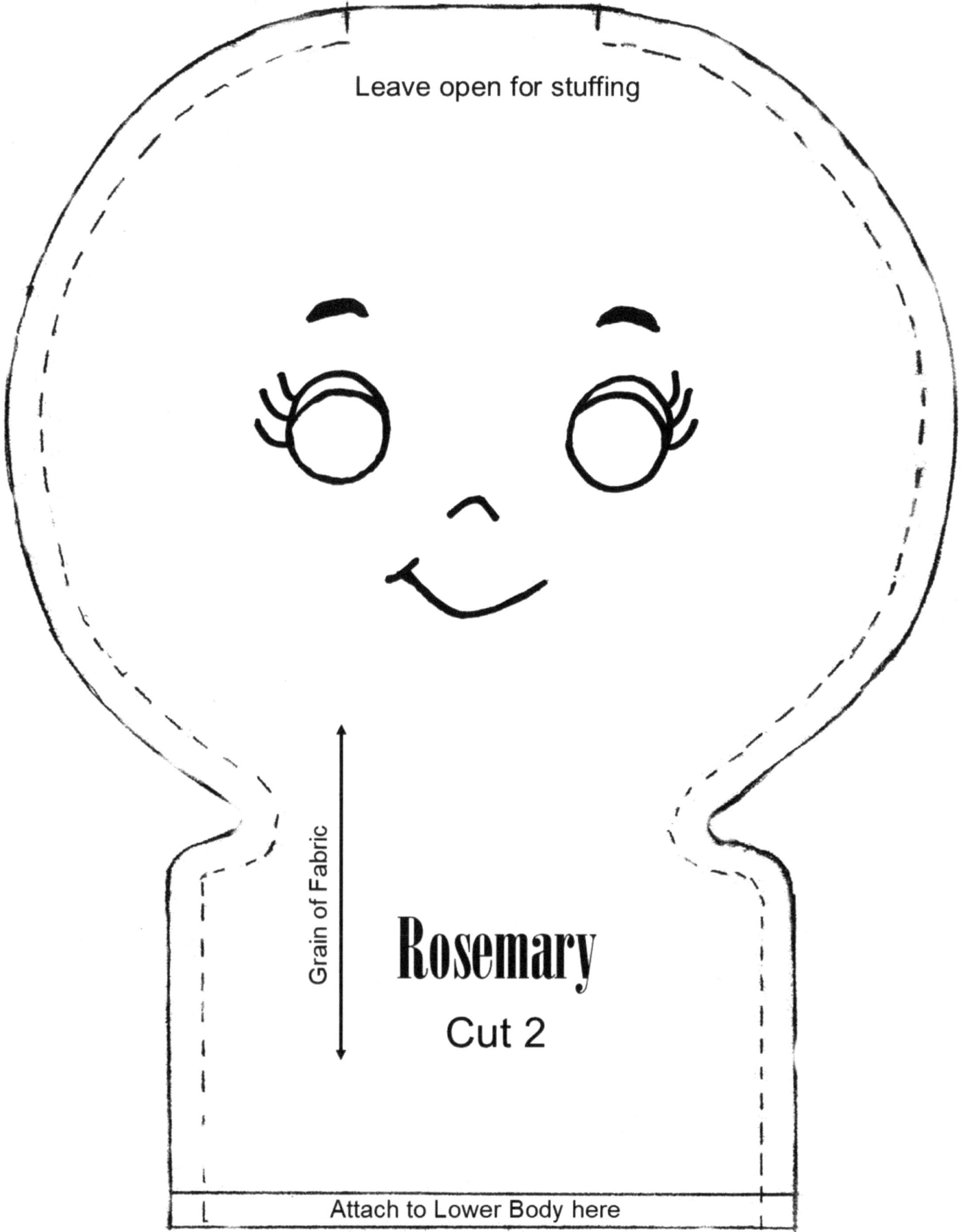

Leave open for stuffing

Grain of Fabric

Rosemary

Cut 2

Attach to Lower Body here

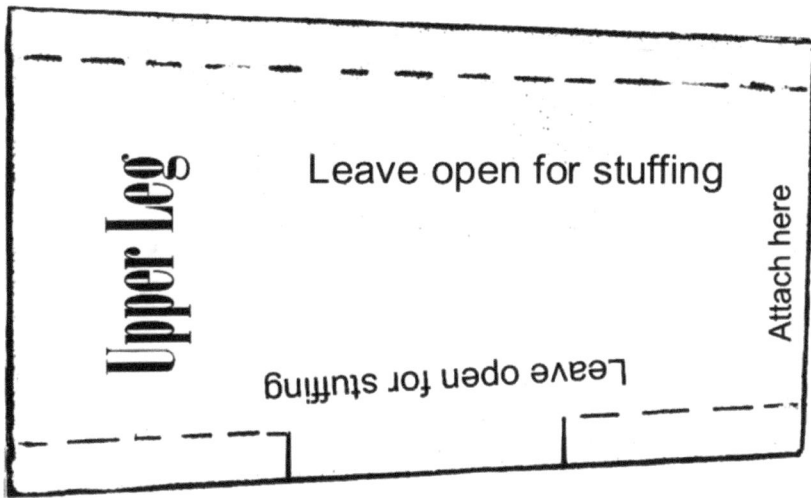

Upper Leg

Leave open for stuffing

Leave open for stuffing

Attach here

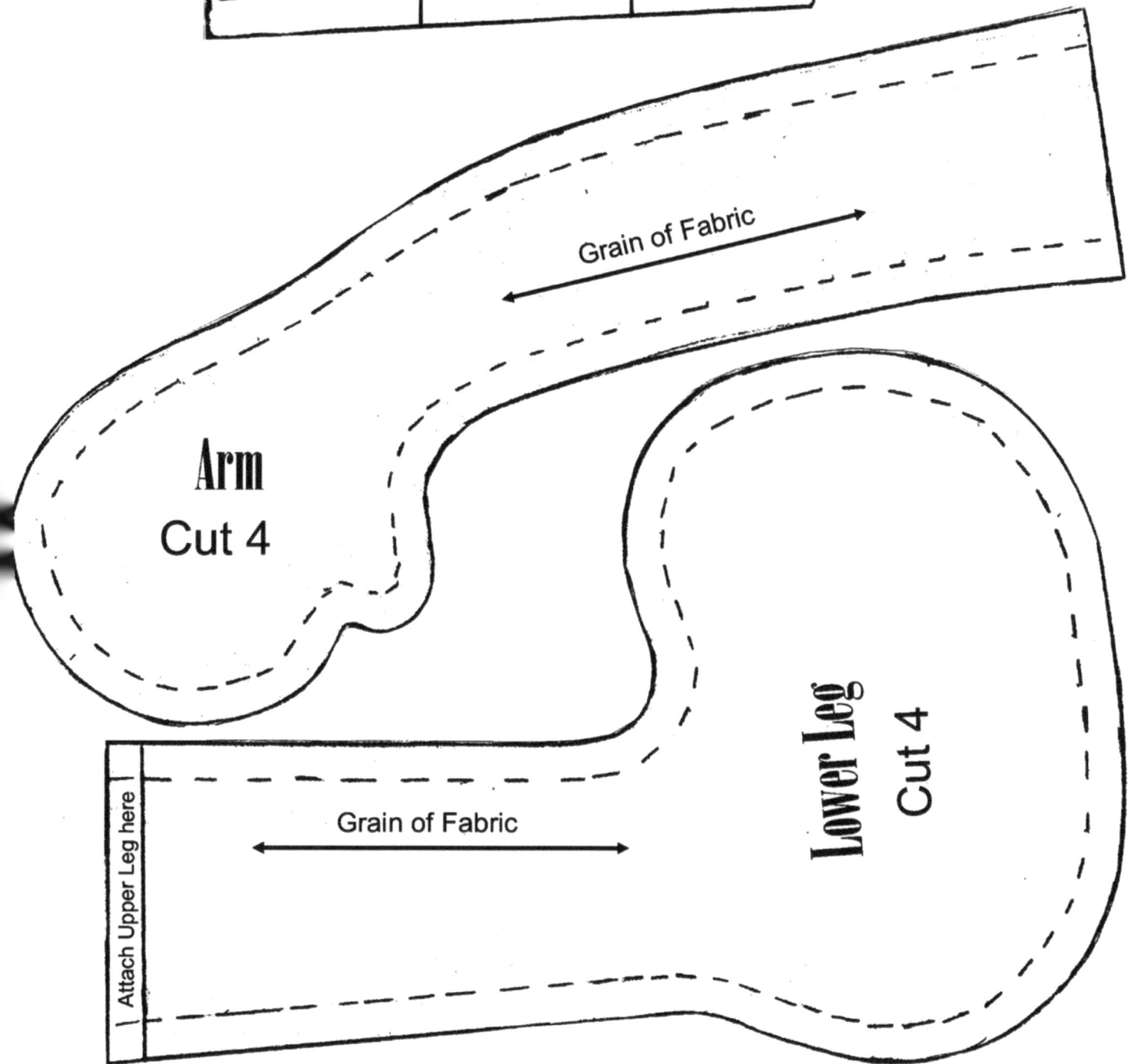

Arm

Cut 4

Grain of Fabric

Lower Leg

Cut 4

Grain of Fabric

Attach Upper Leg here

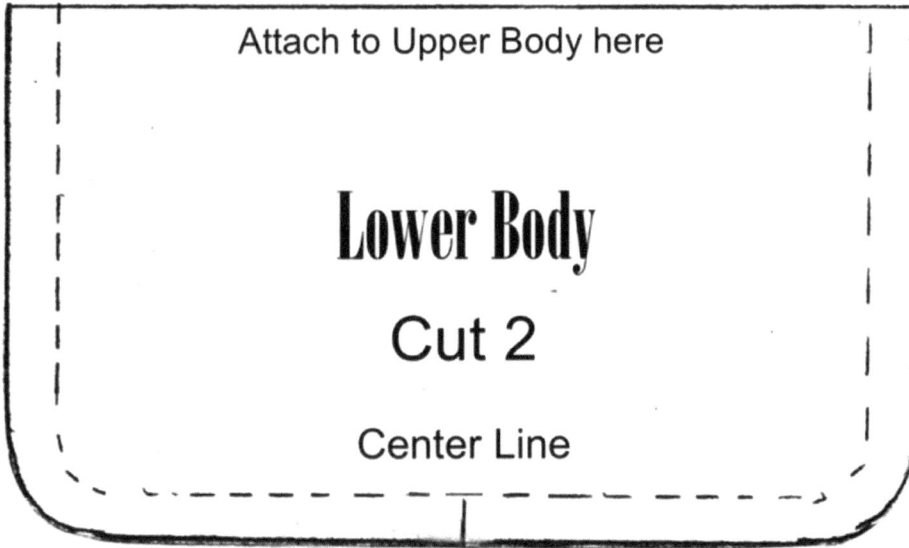

Attach to Upper Body here

Lower Body

Cut 2

Center Line

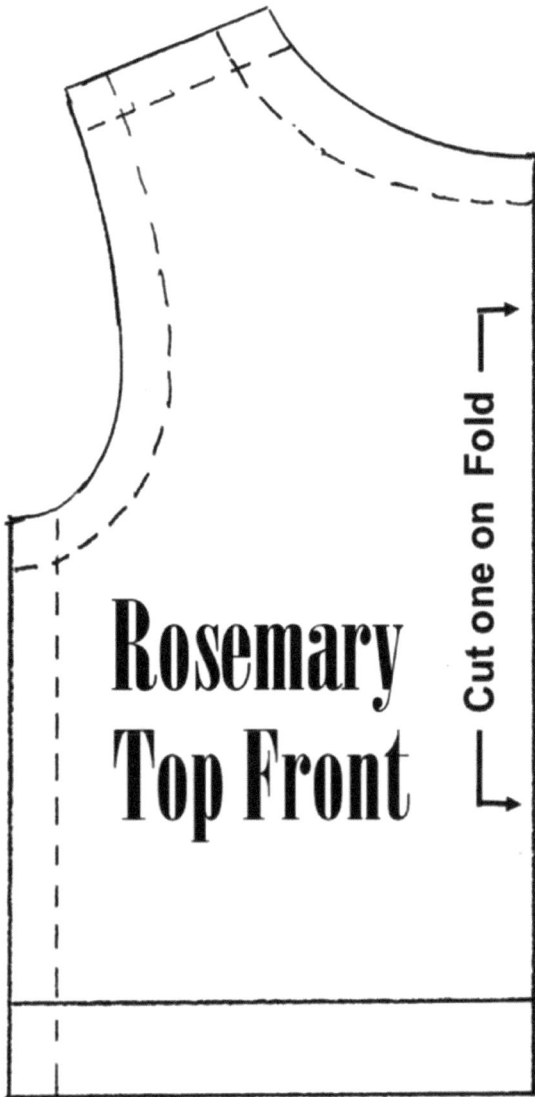

Rosemary
Top Front

Cut one on Fold →

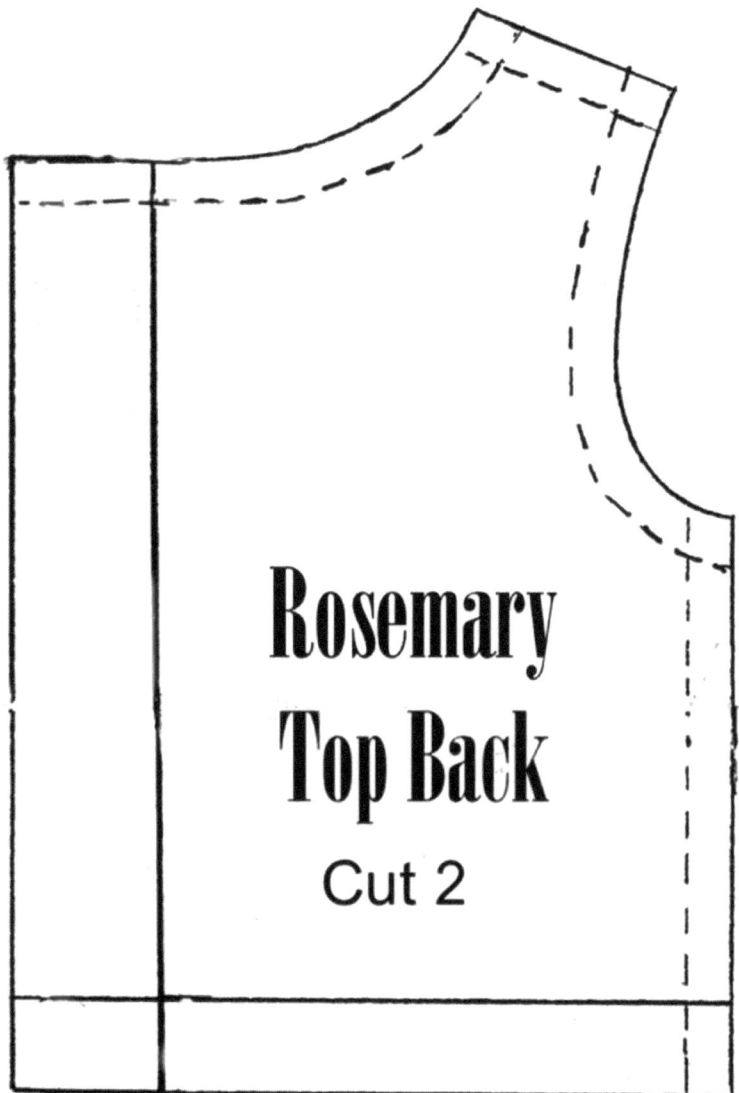

Rosemary
Top Back

Cut 2

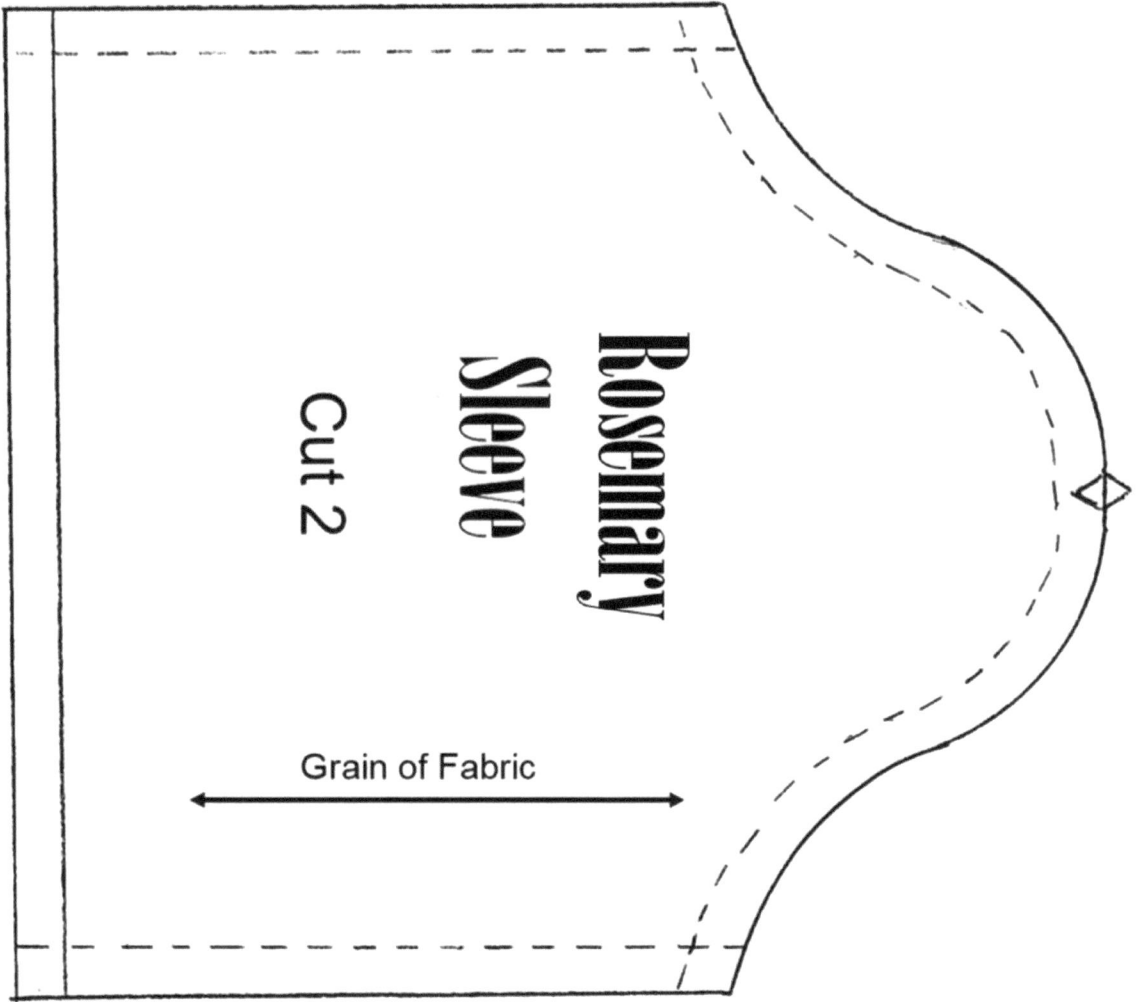

Rosemary Sleeve

Cut 2

Grain of Fabric

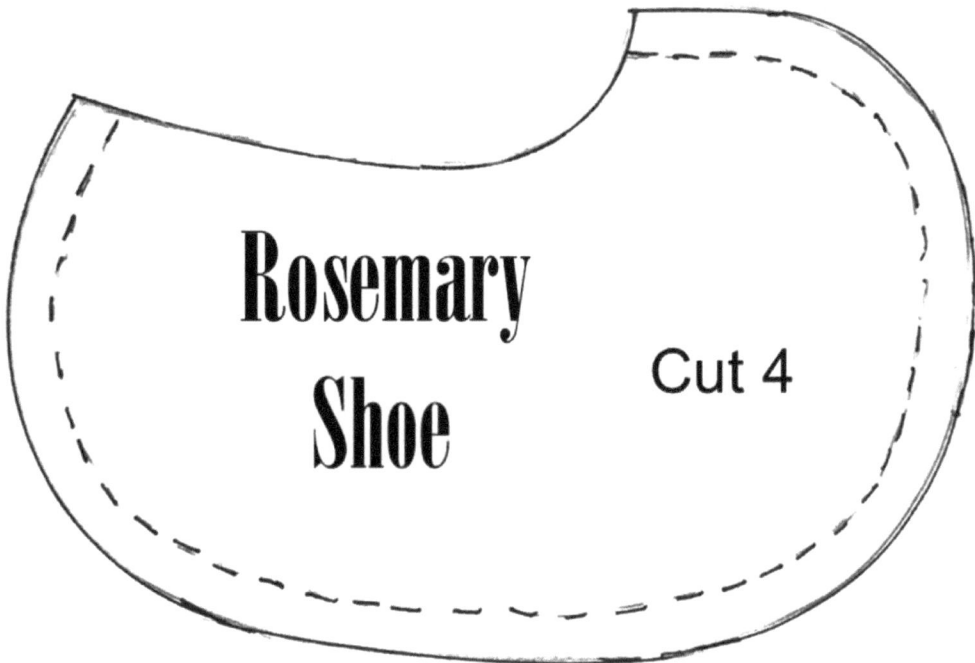

Rosemary Shoe

Cut 4

Fold for Casing for Waist Elastic

Attach to Skirt Back here

Rosemary
Skirt Front

Cut 1 on Fold

Add Trim here

Back Seam

Rosemary
Skirt Back

Attach to Skirt Front here

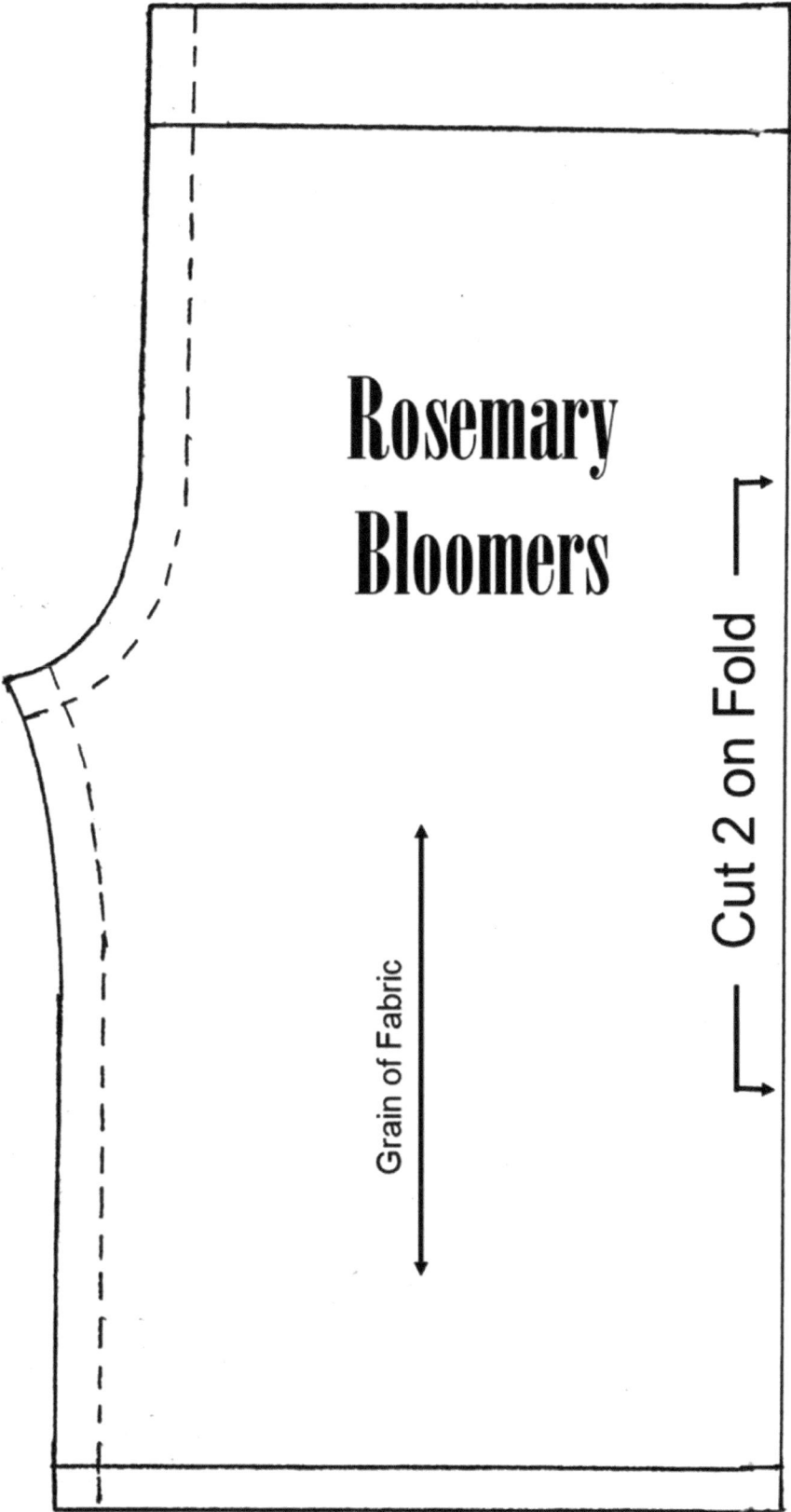

Rosemary Bloomers

Grain of Fabric

Cut 2 on Fold

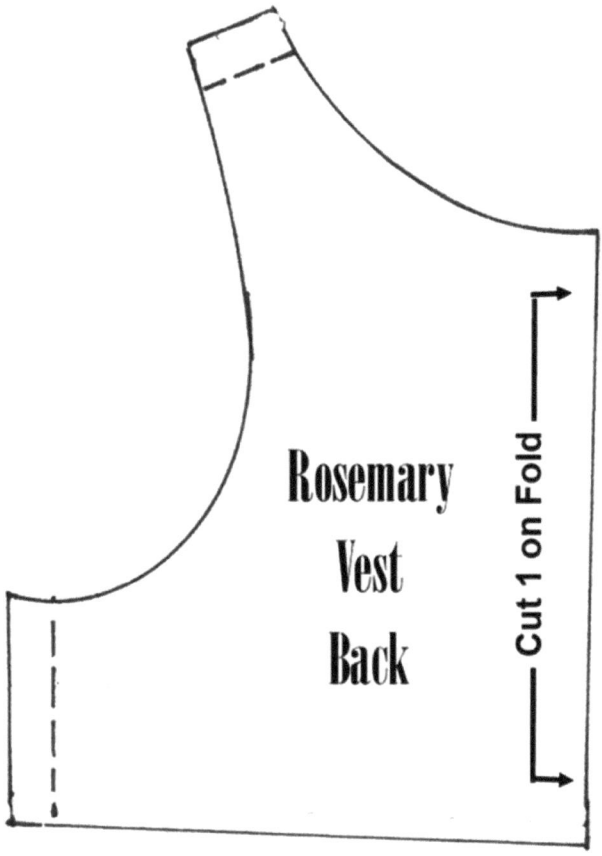

Rosemary
Vest
Back

Cut 1 on Fold

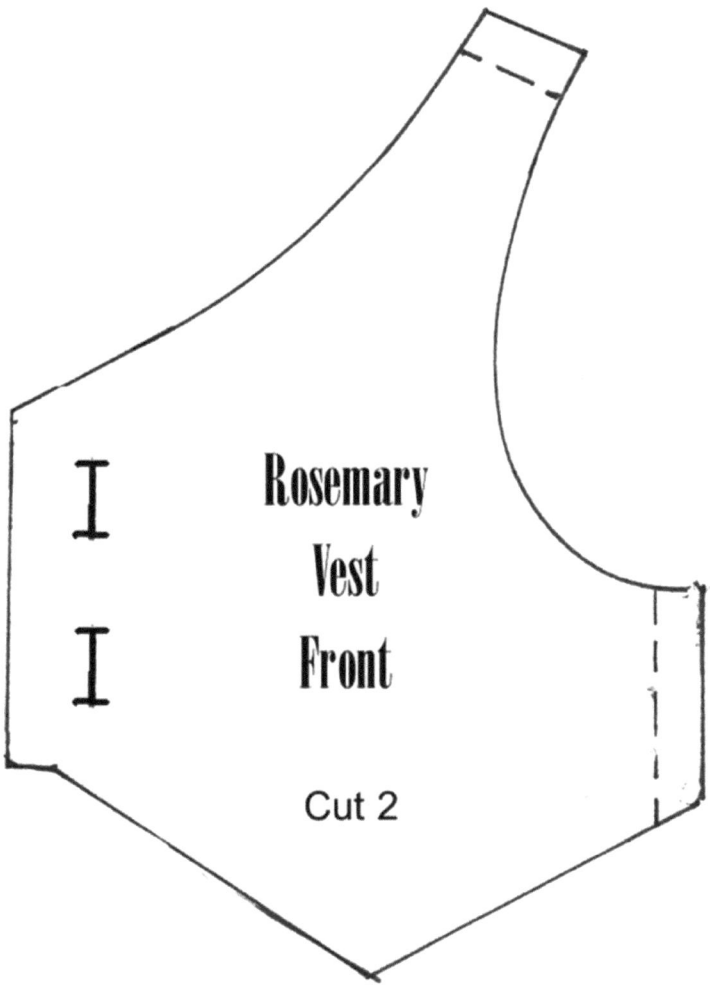

Rosemary
Vest
Front

Cut 2

www.ingramcontent.com/pod-product-compliance
Lightning Source LLC
Chambersburg PA
CBHW041551040426
42447CB00002B/143